THREE RUSSIAN POETS

Three Russian Poets
ELAINE FEINSTEIN

Margarita Aliger
Yunna Moritz
Bella Akhmadulina

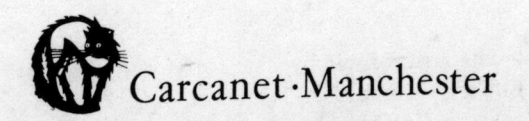

Carcanet·Manchester

Copyright © Elaine Feinstein 1979

SBN 85635 227 6

All Rights Reserved

First published in 1979 by
Carcanet New Press Limited
330 Corn Exchange Buildings
Manchester M4 3BG

The Publisher acknowledges the financial assistance
of the Arts Council of Great Britain.

Printed in Great Britain by
Billings, Guildford

CONTENTS

Introduction / 9

MARGARITA ALIGER
Two lyrics from For a Man on his Way / 19
Great Expectations / 22
'My lips are salt' / 24
Two / 25
To the Portrait of Lermontov / 26
'If everything' / 27
House in Meudon / 28
For Neruda / 31
'Much too happy' / 32

YUNNA MORITZ
Midday in Gantiadi / 35
'In twilight' / 36
In Memory of Francois Rabelais / 37
Three lyrics from Poems for her Sick Mother / 39
'Midnight cold' / 42
Autumn Morning Frost / 43
'Now we'll go' / 45
'The bell' / 46

BELLA AKHMADULINA
A Bad Spring / 49
Winter / 52
Music Lessons / 53
Fever / 55
I Swear / 60
Night / 62
'For how many years' / 64
Twelve lyrics from Rain / 65
Chapters from a Poem / 75
'You were sleeping' / 80

INTRODUCTION

The three poets included in this book do not represent a readily defined group. Aliger belongs to the generation born at the time of the Revolution. Moritz and Akhmadulina came to fame alongside Yevtushenko and Vozhneshensky. All three are women, but their concerns have not been shaped by that any more than those of their great predecessors Anna Akhmatova and Marina Tsvetayeva.

Margarita Aliger was born in 1918 in a poor Jewish family in Odessa. It was a family already assimilated to the main streams of Russian cultural life. Her father played the violin well and composed a little music, though he had no opportunity to develop his talent. He also knew four languages. Her mother read the classics of Russian poetry to her. Such a family naturally supported the Revolution; and certainly Aliger was glad to take the chance of education the new régime offered to study first Chemistry and then Literature in Moscow.

Her poems were published in magazines when she was little more than a schoolgirl; and she soon had a circle of literary friends. Her first husband, however, Constantin Mazakov-Rakitin, was a composer. Aliger worked with him on a libretto for an opera, and they had two children. (The first, a boy, died of meningitis at eight months). Nevertheless, her husband was not the person to whom her most passionate love poems are addressed, and even if he had not been killed in the war, it is doubtful if they would have remained together.

Aliger came to fame in the Soviet Union with the fiercely patriotic poetry she was writing at the outbreak of the Second World War. An epic poem called 'Zoya', about the sufferings of a girl tortured to death by the Nazis was particularly well-known. I have not represented this period of her work here, except for an odd, claustrophobic vision of domestic life under threat in 'Great Expectations'. In a way this poem belies the reality of Aliger's life which was far from cosy. She was, for instance, brave enough to fly into Leningrad at the height of the siege and report the horrors of it and she spent little time at home.

But the war was not only a time of horror and loss for Aliger. It was also the time she was closest to the writer Fadaeev. They never married (Fadaeev already had a wife), but they were lovers and friends for many years, and Aliger's surviving daughter is his. Fadaeev has always been a controversial figure. An outstanding novelist, he acted as Secretary of the Writers Union from 1939 to 1953. Inevitably, while there are stories of writers who were saved by him, there have also been doubts about the role he played in the fate of others. During the last years of his life, Aliger and he were estranged, and Fadaeev began drinking more and more heavily. In 1956 he killed himself. It was in the Autumn of that year that Aliger wrote her short, sad lyric, 'Two'.

Many of Aliger's best lyrics turn upon the unhappiness of being a survivor. It is a theme which has a peculiar poignancy whenever Aliger reflects on the gap between her own generation and that of the younger poets springing up after her whose lives have been so much easier. 'It is because they cannot understand the Thirties, they blame a whole generation together for Stalin's crimes. It was not so simple as they think now,' she said to me. And in a poem dated 1946-56 she writes bitterly: 'People do not forgive me my mistakes'. In Aliger's poem to Lermontov (a poem I much admire) she is writing not only about the difference in fate between her life and that of the great poet who died young, but offering the apology of a survivor, who feels that the price of survival has been to live through more than anyone could be expected to endure.

She is now a short, frail, dark-skinned woman of about sixty, who lives alone in a gracious flat opposite the Tretyakov gallery. Recently Yevtushenko wrote a poem about her called 'Poet in a market' in which he described her going to buy honey for her elder daughter who was in that year very ill, and has since died. He saw in her frail figure standing among 'the cabbages and the lard' unrecognized by other shoppers someone who carried

INTRODUCTION

> the pure light
> and pride of
> someone who was both Jewish woman
> and Russian poet.

Aliger has lived through, and understands at first hand, one of the most cruelly difficult periods of Soviet history. In 1976 she said to me that in spite of all the hardships she endured then she had probably been happiest during the Second World War, because 'It was the time when all our people were together, and knew they were fighting an enemy *outside* that was evil.'

Aliger was on the same train as Akhmatova, travelling towards Chistopol in 1941. She remembers someone commenting on the beads Anna Akhmatova was wearing round her neck. 'That was a present from Marina,' Akhmatova said. And everyone fell silent, appalled by the knowledge of Tsvetayeva's suicide two months earlier, in the little town of Yelabuga, on the river Kama. The question of guilt preoccupies Aliger. In her memoir of Akhmatova, she tells the story, and wonders whether it is possible to ask who is guilty. Aliger, with Tsvetayeva's daughter Alya, and Ilya Erenburg, has been among the most hard-working of the Commission set up to re-establish Tsvetayeva's reputation (and indeed publication) in Russia. Quite recently, Aliger's long brooding over Tsvetayeva's suicide brought her to write one of her own finest poems: 'House in Meudon'.

All through her life, Aliger has seen the writing of poetry as primarily a means of sharing the experiences of pain and joy with other people. In her most recent poems her conversational manner has become more terse and even more direct. The political changes that have affected her life most deeply over forty years of writing are now most movingly expressed in poems of love and mourning.

The gap between generations can be felt as we move from Margarita Aliger, to Yunna Moritz, who (like Akhmadulina) was only a child in the war that was the central experience of Aliger's life. Apart from Akhmadulina, Yunna Moritz is unquestionably the most widely praised of contemporary women poets. The personality of the two women is very different. Akhmadulina is flamboyant, even reckless in manner, stylishly dressed, with a black-eyed, high-cheeked beauty. Yunna Moritz has a pale, long face, sad grey eyes and a gentle voice. She speaks quietly and slowly, as if she is thinking out her answers for the first time. When she reads, she avoids the rhetoric of public delivery, preferring to sound more like a person reading aloud to herself. She is also much more mysterious and difficult to reach as a person, not so much out of a desire to *hide*, but out of a genuine hatred of the explicit. Moritz was a great favourite of Akhmatova's, and other poets have compared the quality of her nature poetry to Pasternak's. When I spoke to her in 1977 in Moscow, however, she refused to see herself in terms of literary influence. She introduced herself to me with the sentence: 'I am a very strange poet'. And she preferred to speak of the influence not so much of other writers as of whole cultures and periods, particularly the Baroque, which I took to mean the profusion of imagery at once rich and homely that fills her poems. She has a great love for the richness of the earth, and the people of the South with their exotic traditions of cookery. It seemed however, that she meant rather more than this by the baroque impulse in her poem 'In Praise of Rabelais'. This is a poem which brings together a belief in the immortality of the soul, the releasing power of laughter, and her own sense of an anthill existence, in which men and women live on the false expectation that things must be gradually improving. When she claims in this poem that it is within the sacred power of laughter to make us find the most tragic facts of this world *comic*, it is a hard-won, tough and personal knowledge, which ignores nothing.

For Yunna Moritz was born in 1937 in Kiev, of Jewish parentage, and must be counted lucky to have survived the massacres that attended Hitler's first drive into Russian territory. Nevertheless, her first collection of poetry was published when she was only twenty; and in 1964 she chose to publish a collection of translations from the Jewish poet

M. Toif. Her life has been hard in many ways. She has suffered from tuberculosis. Her husband, a literary critic, committed suicide at the time of the Russian invasion of Czechoslovakia. Even now, though her reputation stands high among writers, she is not widely enough published to enjoy the grand style of life that the Writers Union can offer its successful poets. Nor is her work yet at all well-known outside the Soviet Union, (though there are excellent translations of her work in Daniel Weissbort's *Post-War Russian Poetry*). I am conscious that there ought to be a far larger section of her work in this book. She is unquestionably an extremely difficult poet to translate, however; partly because her use of surprising words and images draws so strongly upon the resonant music of the Russian language; and even more because of an allusive elliptical manner, which loses all its pressure if a translator tries to present only straightforward meaning.

I find Yunna Moritz at her best when she is most movingly simple, as in the two poems for her sick mother which she read to me in Moscow first explaining: 'I'd like to admit these poems are based on real facts from my own life... but nevertheless they are also concerned with a universal human terror.'

Bella Akhmadulina was born in Moscow in 1937, with Italian and Tartar ancestors. Her striking beauty and her warm, affectionate presence hide an almost febrile intensity. In Pavel Antokosky's Introduction to her 1975 collection he speaks of Akhmadulina's 'strong masculine talent... I don't mean in the craftsmanship, or technique... but where it really matters, at the root; in the moral tension of a human being who is growing, even as we look. She is a poet, not a poetess.' Many voices would join him in that; and it is , I believe, no accident that it is Bella Akhmadulina who has most boldly taken upon herself the inheritance of her great women predecessors, Anna Akhmatova and Marina Tsvetayeva. Yevtushenko dates her maturity as a poet from the moment she first acknowledged that weight upon her, and singles out particularly her poem 'I Swear'. From that point on, he says, her own nerves became 'the nerves of her age'. That poem he claims was 'an inner Rubicon . . . after which she felt herself nervously responsible for everything that was, is and shall be'. 'I Swear' is a poem in which Akhmadulina personified the murderous forces of bureaucratic pettiness as a fairy-tale monster, to which she gives the name Yelabuga, the town where Marina Tsvetayeva took her own life. When she spoke about the poem to me in 1977, she was at pains to point out that the inhabitants of that particular town were of course innocent.

At her finest, Akhmadulina combines a fierce, comic invention with her most passionate utterance: she turns her wit upon herself (as in 'Fever'), or upon the complacent materialism of the worldly (in 'A Fairy Tale of Rain'), with equal ferocity. Her voice often recalls that of Tsvetayeva in 'Praise to the Rich'. In many of her poems the figure of the poet is compelled to behave in ways that bring the contempt of more conventional people upon him.

When I met Akhmadulina in Paris, I asked her whether she felt that her poetic gift was a kind of curse.

> I am not sure it would be quite accurate to say that. What is more important to me is the state I experience when I write . . . I think whenever a gift is given to a human being it affects her fate, or her gift is affected by her fate. Particularly a poet. Perhaps a poetic gift does sentence whoever has it to some kind of grief or doom. Sometimes I do feel it a heavy burden. And I say to myself, I don't want to write. But I have never been able to stop . . . Sometimes when young people come to me for advice I tell them . . . If you're able not to write, then stop. The only valid reason for writing is the total inability to live without doing so.

Nothing could be more like Tsvetayeva's own words, in her essay 'Art in the Light of Conscience', where she describes poetry at its greatest as a kind of possession 'to which the poet must abandon himself, as Blok did when he wrote *The Twelve* in a single night and got up in complete exhaustion, like one who has been driven upon'.

At the centre of 'A Fairy Tale of Rain', another heroine who feels herself to belong to a world of values ignored in her society finds herself pursued by Rain, which takes many shapes, but always suggests the playful fertility of the human spirit. Whether Rain is the gift of poetry or poetry itself, its one determination is to prevent the heroine making a peaceful adjustment to the arid materialism she feels on every side. She has an invitation to a party at a house of considerable splendour, where she knows she will meet hidden disapproval, precisely because she cannot be trusted to behave conventionally. She will be tolerated only because she has a certain fashionable reputation. But the discomfort is mutual. The heroine senses something sinister in the beauty of this house; a corruption in its very perfection of taste. When at last she rings the bell and appears, soaked by the rain, the guests try to bring her close to the fire to dry out. Akhmadulina imagines in their invitation an echo of that medieval hatred and fear of the strange that once had led people to burn witches. Akhmadulina often works best within the context of an extended metaphor. Although many of her short lyrics are tender, she needs space and length to let her voice rise to its true pitch, as it does in the climax of 'Rain'.

Although a psychological affinity with Tsvetayeva accords with the speed and flow of Akhmadulina's poetry, and is clearly very much stronger, Akhmadulina has always honoured Akhmatova deeply as she explained to me in Paris, before telling me an extremely funny story about one of their rare meetings. It seems Bella once offered to drive Akhmatova to her *dacha*. Unfortunately, Bella's car stalled at traffic lights; and the journey ended ignominiously with Akhmatova firmly refusing even the offer of a lift in Bella's friend's car with the decisive words: I never make the same mistake twice.

In spite of this irreverent account, Akhmadulina explains

the reason for the remoteness of her acquaintance with Akhmatova in a very characteristic way.

> I had immeasurable love and respect for Anna Andreevna but I am so organized internally that I never try to meet the people I love so much. It was the same with Pasternak. I loved Akhmatova's poetry so much I could not think of any kind of relationship between us. The distance between Akhmatova and Tsvetayeva and—myself—is enormous. I love them both far more than I love myself.

She goes on to refuse the comparison between her poetry and theirs; but there must be many who share with me Yevtushenko's belief that she is very much in the tradition of the two great woman poets who stand over her shoulder.

I should like to acknowledge with gratitude literal versions provided for the poems of Bella Akhmadulina by Bernard Comrie and Patrick Miles, and for those of Margarita Aliger and Yunna Moritz provided by Richard Davies, who was also responsible for the literal version of Akhmadulina's 'You were sleeping'.

Margarita Aliger

Two lyrics from
FOR A MAN ON HIS WAY

    I.

I want to be your love
I want to be your strength
fresh wind
          daily bread
sky flying overhead

a path under your feet,
if you should lose your way
use it and don't look back;
if you grow tired and thirsty
look, I become a stream:
come close, bend down, and drink.

If you should want to rest
some night in the darkness
of mountainside or forest,
like smoke from a hut I'll rise
flare up   a flower of fire:
you'll recognise me there.

I will gladly turn myself into
whatever you love in the world;
at dawn, look out of your window,
I'll be in whatever you see.

I will turn into a bird
(an iridescent tom-tit)
singing   at the day's end.
Yes, you must notice me,

there in the turning notes
of the nightingale
                in the leaves.

Can you see dew in those petals?
It is I.
                       And the cloud
hanging above the garden.   Happy?
Then somewhere nearby
my love protects you.

I recognized you among many.
Now our paths are joined.
Do you understand, my love?
Wherever you are you will meet me.
You cannot help but see me.
You'll have to love me for ever!

VI.

I do not want to meet you in the winter.
    You will always live in my soul as you were
in the springtime, with an uncovered head on
    that happiest day of my life, as in a dream.

I do not want to meet you in the winter.
    I am afraid of finding you older and drier,
of hearing you quarrel with your wife
    and seeing your indifference to a friend;

I'm afraid to discover that you can be
    bored, even for a moment, or finding out
you turn your collar up, like anyone else
    hurrying along under rainy clouds.

I want to remember you forever
    as my friend, my travelling companion,
loving mountains and cities, roads and rivers
    insatiably, always carefree, wonderstruck.

So, live like that. As I remember you,
   a man of impulses and nervous tension,
go on loving animals and trees.
   Know much, but go on asking many questions.

Look far ahead now in the distance
   with your transparent, wandering eyes.
Sometimes I feel at ease only to remember
   whatever else, that you are still alive.

So, while the day lasts, while the rivers flow
   rushing by in froth, I dream of
keeping you   exactly as you were then,
   how you were and how I'll always love you.

And even if I have invented you
   (a man that I should most desire to meet)
I do not want to have the fiction shattered.
   I do not want to meet you in the winter.

GREAT EXPECTATIONS

    The flame of kerosene flickers.
        Alone in the house with Dickens:
    ... in the darkness around us burn
        fires of *Great Expectations*.

    O how deeply he longed for
        happiness, poor young Pip!
    ... This house without noise
        is filled with the gloom of war.

    Is it so long since voices
        brightened the home with sound?
    Pain has not blinded me.
        I can see the distant sails,

    and feel the golden freedom,
        not yet throttled by sadness.
    ... It is the end of forty one.
        The Nazis close on Moscow.

    The nearby battle booms
        (all expectations rising)
    in Petrichshevskaya square
        Zoya goes to her death.

    We cannot save her from torture,
        give her some water or help.
    The guns blaze all around us.
        The night of siege is hollow.

    Alarming the outline of buildings:
        no chink of light shows there:
    the only ray that warms us
        is the light of great expectations.

My bitter love, where are you?
    Come back into my verse!
I'm already losing the marks
    of the threads that you tore loose.

Only the memory of early days
    brightens this cruel end,
that summer flash of expectation
    when we trembled like captives together.

Whatever comes upon us,
    whatever the days bring,
I remember poor young Pip
    and those fires of *Great Expectations*!

With everything changed, inside out;
    everything hurtful and bitter,
with the flight of great expectations
    something still strains forward.

Bad times are strangely similar
    whenever they strike home.
. . . It is the end of forty one.
    The Nazis close on Moscow.

At the time of sharpest pain
    some star of great expectations
familiar from our childhood
    always appears for everyone

and the path towards it looks
    comforting however steep.
Perhaps even great achievements
    pale beside   great expectations!

'My lips are salt'

My lips are salt, and my eyelashes.
　　I have forgotten nothing:
no grief, no happiness is lost
　　of all that has happened to us.

There were no lies, no lies,
　　no treachery or dishonour!
Along a path through rye
　　near Moscow we walked together,

in a small field of bluebells
　　we once sat on the grass;
from the steep bank of a hill,
　　we watched carp in the river.

Centuries-old oaks bearing
　　extremes of heat and snow
all know the story of our fate
　　and tell it to one another.

Above the River Moskva
　　you cannot guess the distance
or measure all the earth we walked
　　once on those hills together.

And when we part for the last time
　　(that is, when life is over),
the sound of our feet and hearts
　　will still be heard by people

who may inherit all our
　　light-blue earth, and sunset glow
this morning wind across the fields,
　　and apple-blossom snow!

As we loved one another there
　　let them love　　whoever they are!

TWO

Once again they've quarrelled on a tram,
    shamelessly indifferent to strangers.
I can't hide how much I envy them.
    I can't take my eyes off their behaviour.

They don't even know their good fortune,
    and not knowing is a part of their luck.
Think of it. They are together. Alive.
    And have the time to sort things out and make up.

TO THE PORTRAIT OF LERMONTOV

My twenty-six year old ensign,
please forgive me, please forgive
the twice as many years I've lived
in this bright world, where I still am.
Forgive me, please forgive me, for
every feast and every day, it's
been my fortune to have more,

twice as many more than you!
And yet if I've had twice your days
there has been room in them for twice
as many fears and injuries.
Who knows which century it was
easier to bear? Between us
who was luckier? What weighs more,
heavy blows the living feel, or
grass that's growing overhead?

You don't answer since you're dead.
And I won't answer. I'm alive . . .

'If everything'

If everything I cannot learn to bear
    could only be turned into a
song or a story with a firm line
    the weight of grief would leave my heart at once,

as other people, men or women, share
    my pain, and help me to live through it.
This is why I first became a poet.
    I can't think of any other reason.

HOUSE IN MEUDON

Grey and dingy house in Meudon,
dull and grey old house in Meudon,
flat as board   four storeys high
uncoloured brick, unlit, unchosen
there by someone else's garage, like
a burnt-out candle, dripping wax:
there it was you lived, Marina.

Grey and dingy house in Meudon.
Nothing grows on that verandah.
There's no smile behind the window,
just a dead house, stiff with cold, with
no dogs, no cats and alone
deserted like a bivouac.

How long since the Russian language
was used there? To cry or laugh or
hide your misery from children,
suffer in,   or breathe, or be
written in notebooks until morning.
Now this upright narrow house
has fallen into French silence
with its gates closed at the bend.
It conjures up by day and night
all your memories in my heart.

From now on, to move or not, will
alter nothing. Magic cannot
change the bends that wait for you
hollows ahead, and more mirages—
houses by other people's garages.

Now I have it on my palm,
in my own hands: the dingy house.
Look, how bare it is, how lonely,
always facing down the road
three hundred metres. To the station.

—I must pack my bundle now.
—What's the hurry? Off to Paris?
What's the fever? What's the panic?
You've seen Berlin once already.
Do you want to go to Prague?
—No. I'd rather die. I'll go to
no more foreign cities. Ever.

I must go back to Trekhprudny,
to Granatny, Plyushikha, the Arbat . . .
Yes, let's be going. Soon, as soon
as can be. Fast. At a run.
Still the dingy house in Meudon—
Stubbornly, its black stare follows.
While you find your last dark river
Kama, rocks, insects, and that
small town that reaches down the hill.

To the Kama, then, from Meudon.
To be without a home or foothold.
Not to prison. Not to freedom.
With a great stone in your throat.
Two years. No address. No shelter.
Without a word. Without a word.
Without daughter. Without husband.
Only horror, hard frost, sirens,
and the war shriek overhead.

Still your son was with you, in that
wooden hut above the river.
Who was guilty then? Of what?
In that dark house, on that rough road.

All around you, Russia, Russia
danced in golden rings barefoot
in the small woods
                    on the steep banks,

Russia who had brought you up
a daughter once—then let you go.
So, did you displease her? How?
Because you went away from home
and lost yourself in foreign lands?
That she forgave you long ago.
Russia had not time, not then,
to understand you, all her women
wept in all the villages,
wagons always on the move
steppes on fire, and all her people
running away. How could she then
remember you? Or bother with you?
There you were. Behind the fence.
Yelabuga. The edge of war.
For no fault of yours forgotten.
Mother Russia. Mother Rus'.
This cold. Bleak. I am afraid.

What comes next Lord? Every August
is the end of summer. So
what happens? Every year
rains come and the hardest clay
erodes and crumbles. Winter comes.
Marina. How will you live through it?
The Kama will not move. No way
to cross. By foot or horse. No path
Or road. Only the snow. Blizzard.
No friend. Not even an enemy.
Only snow and snow and snow
like our landlady's featherbed!
You won't be able to leave the yard.
Marina. How will you live through it?
Even you can't handle this.
You've gone too far.
—Yes. This is it.
              And your last trick?
                      A hempen rope.

FOR NERUDA

    Massive, heavy, with a small Kepi
        on his large head, dressed in
    a well-cut suit, (well-made at least
        to make its owner comfortable)
    so: he is massive, heavy, strong,
        an undisturbed man and reliable,
    who lives wherever he is as if
        in every cell of his body, every minute,
    he thinks, acts, walks and breathes like
        a sailor or a miner or a lumber-jack
    or perhaps an aristocrat.
    What he most resembles
    is a stone, from his native shore, a stone
        that has rolled down from the Cordillera
    on the line between sea and sand;
        a stone, which time and wind and
    the great ocean waves have given
        an intricate form   which is improbable
    at heart   and yet altogether human.

'Much too happy'

>Much too happy always
>in the strength of your love
>I see now, much too late,
>that after all I was stronger.
>I had the strength to bear it
>all,   for as long as needed.
>When you were most cruel
>you were really begging for help.
>Everything could have been saved
>if I had taken it on!
>And there's no one to say 'forgive me'
>to now   since you are gone.
>The powerless words burn
>my lips. What's the use?
>>   And why
>do people still declare
>that I am left alive!

Yunna Moritz

MIDDAY IN GANTIADI

His eyelids are dark as coffee, the Southerner,
who has taken pancakes stuffed with lamb from
the hot meat dish in the cauldron,
and the sexual charm in his smile is
as calm as the life of a vegetable
or the brown flesh of Greek olives.

He draws me secretly towards him, as if
by oil of camphor-wood, or some
insidious attraction without name,
older than the power of any reptile
and more abrupt than a pirate attack,
as if he was marked out in metal for me.

It is wrong to evade what you know,
as black ravens do if their path
should happen to cross the path of a bat;
forget your finicky pretence
of working miracles, though you long for them,
and always go to sleep in their light,

because you will wake again in idleness
and not be morally outraged, your spirit has
already been initiated.
Drink the Muscatel, gulp down
its fragrance from your chipped cylinder.
And for your sin?—hope only for forgiveness!

'In twilight'

In twilight, in smells of whitewash,
    of housepaint, and of lime,
we drink a sparkling tropical tea
    beneath wet-wood scaffolding.

The painters and the carpenters
    have gone at least until morning;
on one elbow in an armchair
    Autumn drinks tea with us, leaning.

To put a house in repair
    is a test of heart and wit,
a frame of mind that brings back
    an image of hospital life.

A freezing sadness, sterile as
    a long needle enters my breast,
my soul feels the very pain of
    flesh drawn in by a thread!

It takes a jerk to return to
    courage and commonsense,
and to numb that part of me
    which responds yet remains unquenchable.

But so it is, in Florence,
    a piano begins to play for us
marvellous threepart inventions
    of Johann Sebastian Bach.

IN MEMORY OF FRANCOIS RABELAIS

To lie at the edge of the forest
with your face in the earth is miraculous
for idleness is tender, and
can be possessed entirely
in vegetable joy just as
bees sing into clover.

Feel the space under the planet.
Hold on to grass and beetles.
Gulp down the smell of the zoo
on your own skin. We live among
fair booths, where time is short,
packed in together densely.

In paradise no more idols!
People do what they like
joyfully, bathing and lazing,
without any thought of manners.
The healthy spirit of Rabelais
rules the whole population there.

No better world to wait for!
Laughter rises easily
and stories. Pierrot can
dance on his drum as naked
as if he were in a bath-house.
The show is for everyone.

When laughter beats in your ears,
your soul knows it's immortal.
The freedom is like a mouthful
of wine   a breathing space
a forgetting of this life's brevity.
The saddest truth can be funny.

Now go back to your anthill,
put coffee on the stove there.

Chew at your greens for supper.
Enjoy the simplest flavour,
and as you do so savour
the strangeness of carrying on!

Once you can shout and laugh
like a monkey at death and fate
and how men and women act—
the pause is wholly blessed.
A laugh is the outrageous sign
that your soul remains alive.

Unhealthy fevers shake us
in this stern world. Tormented,
by chasing after success,
we may lose all we possess.
Even our souls may leak away
then, and only return to us
with Hell and horned beasts!

Three lyrics from
POEMS FOR HER SICK MOTHER

   I.

Whiteness   the whiteness of these skies
heavily clamping down over our bodies;
when the time comes our souls will pass through you
only too easily. So here I am, Lord,
blocking my mother's entrance to paradise
ready to curse the light blue roof of it
however you harass me into the cracks
like a snake   I won't give her up to you yet
gnawing stones and howling where I sit.
And I refuse to let my mother past.

   II.

Misfortune is as huge
and heavy as this cold
I'm half-dead. Without home.
Without a roof   or wing

Alone under bare skies.
A stump of birchwood chair
my table drowned by rain
abandoned, covered in snow.

My pages rustled through
by icy winds. Mother!
Snow-girl. Small bird.
Snow-girl. Don't touch the fire!
The bonfire. Lie quite still.
Like a water drop on sand
like a red tear on my cheek.
Don't touch! Lie quite still.

Don't touch the fire. Lie there.
Perhaps death will hold back.
And spring will come. Spring!
With peas and beans returning
a star will fall in the well
or a single drop of dew.
Spring birds where are you flying?
A frail old woman can so easily
dwindle away to nothing
before you return. It's hard not to!

I wait in the hospital courtyard
and sitting here make up my prayer.
Trees. Trees. Lake. Lake.
While there is time to spare
before my mother's small body is bruised
yellow and blue. Please. Give me
a small piece of spring, whose
time will come anyway, spring always comes:
beans appear, peas come up,
and small prickly cucumbers.
I won't believe it, I won't believe it. No.

It is impossible mother should go
for ever   before the first strawberries.
And yet the stars are bright over the fields.
There is snow in the wind over the poplars.
Against the wall a snowdrift. Like a breast.
And we are children. Grant us a little spring!

V.

A flight of birds has arrived in
their many-coloured coats.
In the yard, grass is thick
like fur on a baby bear—
on a green bear, yes, a green one,

the smallest and the youngest bear.
People are walking about,
and animals. Bless all walkers!
Look, the city will survive,
every village will survive.
For the sun will shine in
the light blue heights again.
The pear will come to fruit,
like potato, like wheat . . .
And Mother is learning to walk.

Don't fall, don't fall, little tear,
it mustn't be slippery for her!

'Midnight cold'

Midnight cold of oxygen
bronze vitriol of stars:
spirals of scorching roses
are kindled around my window

and nobody moves along
the empty path in the distance
where I see a tall shadow,
too tall for any human.

I recognize the Muse.
Her steps sing every syllable.
At the sound, roses break loose
and float down to her feet.

Her wide stare is serious
her lips are full and firm.
Look how she moves right through
that splendid thought—a bush—

to be lit up by a storm
even as she walks the clouds
bearing a dark-red parcel
of roses in toil-worn hands.

AUTUMN MORNING FROST

I wake up, cold and dark. In Moscow
the radiators are not yet heated. Boreas
blows in from outside the door, where
cats and dogs go numb with cold, and the wind
has long ago pulled out cereals and flowers
with its pincers from the fields and streets.
My hands freeze on the blanket.
My dawn thoughts form without tenderness
into clouds on a mountain, or
dark herds clutched in autumn boredom.
I am like some hero carefully hiding
the way his feelings have darkened with absence.
I observe every sound, every sign.
Above the tin-plate roofs, a sheet which
clattered all night like a stutterer,
now twined up, makes the sound of a heavy kiss.
I wake up. To decipher the habits
of the spirit in a savage mood of gloom.
I wake up. The sky in the east
is as dark as a boarded-up barn.
The troughs of crumbly gutters are
tormented by the noise of shrieks and barks.
I know this place. It's Paradise.
Sit face to face. Run your fingers over
the strings of the Orphic lyre.
Breathe diligently through the dullest lesson.
Domestic noises of laundry, tidying,
and chopping-up now carry everywhere.
But a child, still flushed with play,
takes a woolly lamb in its hands
and walks along the damp street following
an upright shadow resembling
an arrow   in a great bow.
And the antique sciences whisper
both the bow and the lyre were imagined

by that boy once before in a dark time.
For the world is always one and dual. Another
dimension lives in the background of every sound!

'Now we'll go'

    Now we'll go homeward
       in search of a bed
    in a silver pillar of
       Christmas snow

    and there with one toe
       push the heel of the other
    and so take our boots off
       without any bother:

    then inside the coffee pot
       some strange drink rustles.
    We are reminded
       how no soul is bounded;

    and no talent can be
       a convenient mixture
    of things that we like only:
       but what is best and what is worst.

'The bell'

> The bell in the hollow chapel
> and the bell in the throat of the donkey
> fill me with love.   Such depths
> their beauty opens to me.
>
> Here southern valleys feed on
> mad fruitfulness! Asian teahouse
> noises rise in a garden of
> persimmons, mandarins, *feikhoas*.
>
> How easily work is rewarded with crops here!
> Rather as the herds of those going straight to
> the braziers and bonfires of hell multiply!
> The world after death is another great enterprise!
>
> New accounts for it open. Juice and fat
> begin to flow. Sweet smoke goes up the chimney.
> But we still want our freedom, and long to live
> with nothing to darken our fate, don't we?
>
> Even though the way our days are arranged has
> been exposed to the bone, to the Hiroshima bomb.
> We must hold on, keep going, you must understand,
> without my love your world is unbearable.

Bella Akhmadulina

A BAD SPRING

While the untroubled snows were maintaining
their cold light, determined as metal;
the girl over there kept her shawl on, as
she dreamed of a sloped orange beret,
for she wanted her elbows and knees free
to dance down the street as it thawed,
although April had not yet begun all
the bother of insect and plant life.
To take on the sad work of spring then
a neurotic had to turn madman.

Among curtains of winter, and arrogant
snow-drifts, ice-ploughs, and skaters,
he alone suffered the anger of
spring, with its whims and its rages.

As he opened his windows in haste, like
a man choosing death before prison
or someone who tears off a bandage
because he finds pain a temptation.

What was the matter with him? as he
tore down the blind, was it spirit
or else was it some thyroid defect
that needed assistance from iodine?

What power or force it was ruled him
he did not know, though tradition
declares that he looked for misfortune,
and craved suffering as a blessing.

His cry was: I'm doomed as a sinner,
I am no genius. Therefore
it is useless to take any pride in a
forehead: I'm tending a tumour!

Papers and pens now alarmed him.
He spoke out with desperate boldness.
—Lord, since I am your worst pupil
I shall defile no more paper.

Remote, and morose, he rejected
whatever could offer him pleasure,
so his mind could be sharpened with torment;
his hope—to avoid the mediocre.

Inside him small birds chirped: we won't!
But he stunned their weak beauty by forcing
down alcohol and nicotine
into their throats—with a boot.

Only cursing his temper and home,
he said: strange to wake in the morning!
And what you call comfort there burns me.
It feels like the scorching of hell.

His alien house and his garden, an
inquisitive landlady rented
to him in exchange for consuming
his banquets in everyone's sight.

They fed him and gave him wine, their
whispers held no reproach for him,
because he had come into their humdrum
lives—like the feast of the *corrida*.

In some empty shop selling meat-balls
he would give way to grief, drinking cognac.
His fee in the rooms of the underworld:
his performance as—eccentric poet.

They serve him with food he enjoys there
since some female guest, who is clever
(an art expert) has earned the right to
declare to them all he is suffering.

He certainly suffered! His forehead
had been broken on corners, without his
acquiring the least trace of dignity
or a single unchangeable truth.

He has answered his critics with silence, as
they point at impatience and pride in him.
After all, is a dumb person guilty
if he can't use his larynx for singing?

He can be found in parks, bars or town squares,
perhaps on some station benches.
And at last, with his head down, he speaks
as follows: (at least I'll speak for him.)

—My friends, alas, soon I shall be thirty
and the product of all those years is scant,
my efforts at solitude, absurd to me,
and to judge my own work seems imprudent.

God knows what honours will be given
to whom: but this much I know; to me
will be neither too much, nor too little,
yet I go on until I cease existing.

So what is the sense and the use of this
pain which has scarred me with whiteness?
Will a fleeting sound yet appear to me?
And shall I say—was it all for this?

Then perhaps I shall light my candle,
take my pen, and render thanks to Fate,
recalling just how bad a spring this was:
and then—write a poem about it.

WINTER

Winter, to me your gestures are
    cold and careful; yes, in
winter there is something
    gentle as medicine,

or why else would sickness
    put out trusting hands
into that season, from its own
    torture and darkness?

Weave your magic, then,
    my love, let the kiss
of one curl of ice
    brush over my forehead.

Soon I shall trust any
    deception, and look without fear
into the eyes of dogs, as I
    press close to the trees:

and forgive, playfully, with a
    run, turn and jump; and
after a bout of forgiveness
    forgive again,

become like a winter's day:
    empty and oval, though
in comparison to such
    presence, always small,

I shall turn to nothing, and
    so call over the wall,
not some shadow of myself, but light
    I shall not block at all.

MUSIC LESSONS

Marina, how I love to know that
like everyone else, like me—
who cannot speak now through my frozen throat
because to speak of it is like swallowing ice—
to know that you, a creature of light! of snow!
were like the rest of us, given lessons in music.
And there was a waste of teaching, almost as if
to the sound of laughter and tears among
the gods, a candle had been given rules for glowing.
You and the piano, equally dark
creatures, could not get on together.
Two perfect circles, you touched each other's
foreign language, remotely as deaf mutes.
Sombrely you were drawn together in
that insoluble and hostile encounter:
a piano and you! Stubborn and silent,
the voice of music still weak in you both
Marina, defenceless child, that decided
the matter. What is a piano? It is only
silent and a prisoner until some
friend puts a finger on C sharp.
But you were alone. There was no help for you.
Your music had to be learnt with difficulty:
without troubling the source of your pain,
you had to open yourself to bleed in sound.
Marina, C! C! for childhood,
doh, your destiny! *Doh! Re!* if speech,
doh, for everything that comes afterwards!
As we both leant forward our foreheads in
that universal pose before the piano together,
like you! like you! I grasped the stool, that
merry-go-round of a worthless pedagogue,
to try unwinding the same equator
which has already torn away your beret
and now lies whistling around your head.

Marina, the intention of all this springs from
the beauty of uttering just once and perfectly, the cry:
I am like you! like you! I wanted to
shout that out with joy—but instead, I weep.

FEVER

I must be ill, of course. I've been shivering
for three days now like a horse before the races.
Even the haughty man who lives on my landing
has said as much to me:
Bella, you're shaking!

Please control yourself, this strange disease of yours
is rocking the walls, it gets in everywhere.
My children are driven mad by it, and at night
it shatters all my cups and kitchenware.

I tried to answer him: Yes,
I do tremble,
more and more, though I mean no harm to anyone.
But tell everyone on the floor, in any case,
I've made up my mind to leave the house this evening.

However, I was then so jerked about by
fever, my words shook with it; my legs
wobbled; I couldn't even bring my
lips together into the shape of a smile.

My neighbour, leaning over the banister,
observed me with disgust he didn't hide.
Which I encouraged.
—This is just
a beginning. What happens next, I wonder.

Because this is no ordinary illness. I'm sorry to
tell you, there are as many wild and
alien creatures flashing about in me
as in a drop of water under a microscope.

My fever lashed me harder and harder, and
drove its sharp nails under my skin. It was
something like the rain whipping an
aspen tree, and damaging every leaf.

I thought: I seem to be moving about rapidly
as I stand here, at least my muscles are moving.
My body is out of my control completely.
The thing is freely doing whatever it likes.

And it's getting away from me. I wonder if
it will suddenly and dangerously disappear?
Like a ball slipping out of a child's hand,
or a piece of string unreeling from a finger?

I didn't like any of it. To
the doctor
I said, (though I'm timid with him)
—you know, I'm a proud woman! I can't have my
body disobeying me for ever!

My doctor explained:
Yours is a simple disease,
perhaps even harmless, unfortunately
you are vibrating so fast I can't examine you.

You see, when anything vibrates, as you are,
and its movements are so very quick and small,
the object is reduced, visibly speaking
to—nothing. All I can see is: mist.

So my doctor put his golden instrument
against my indefinite body, and a sharp
electric wave chilled me at once
as if I had been flooded with green fire

and the needle and the scales registered horror.
The mercury began to seethe with violence.
The glass shattered, everything splashed about,
and a few splinters drew blood from my fingers.

—Be careful, doctor, I cried. But
he wasn't worried.

Instead, he proclaimed: Your
poor organism is
now functioning normally.

Which made me   sad. I knew myself to belong
to another norm than he had ever intended.
One that floated above my own spirit only
because I was too narrow for such immensity.

And those many figures of my ordeals had
trained my nervous system so that now
my nerves were bursting through my skin, like old
springs through a mattress, screeching at me.

My wrist was still out of shape with its huge
and buzzing pulse, that always had insisted
on racing greedily: Damn it then, run free, I cried
I'll choke with you, as Neva chokes St Petersburg.

For at night my brain has become so sharp with
waiting, my ear so open to silence, if
a door squeaks or a book drops, then—
with an explosion—it's the end of me.

I have never learnt to tame those beasts
inside, that guzzle human blood.
In my presence, draughts blow under doors!
Candles flare—before I extinguish them!

And one enormous tear is always ready
to spill over the rim of my eyes.
My own spirit distorts everything.
My own hell would corrupt heaven.

The doctor wrote me out a Latin scrip.
The sensible and healthy girl in
the chemists shop was able to read the
music in it from the punctuation.

And now my whole house has been softened by
the healing kiss of that valerian,
the medicine has licked into every
wound I have, with its minty tongue.

My neighbour is delighted, three times he
has congratulated me on my recovery,
(through his children). He has even
put in a word for me with the house management.

I have repaid a few visits and debts already,
answered some letters. I wander about
in some kind of profitable circles.
And no longer keep any wine in my cupboard.

Around me—not a sound, not a soul.
My table is dead, dust hides everything on it.
My blunt pencils like illiterate
snouts, are all lying in darkness.

And like a defeated horse, all my
steps are sluggish and hobbling now.
So all is well. But my nights are
disturbed with certain dangerous premonitions.

My doctor has not yet found me out. However
it will not long be possible to
fool him. He may have cured me once, but
soon I know I shall burn and freeze again.

A snail in its grave of bone I am
for the moment saved by blindness and silence—
but still the horns of sick antennae itch
and will rise up once again from my forehead.

Star-fall of full stops and hyphens, I
summon your shower to me! I want to
die with the silvery goose-flesh of
water nymphs burning in my spine.

Fever! I am your tambourine, strike me
without pity! I shall dance, like
a ballerina to your music, or
live like a chilled puppy in your frost.

So far I haven't even begun to
shiver. No, let's not even discuss that. Yet
my observant neighbour is already
becoming rather cold to me when we meet.

I SWEAR

  by that summer snapshot taken
on someone else's porch, skewed to one
side, that looks so like a gibbet, and
points a way out of the house not into it;
where you are wearing some violent sateen dress that
cramps the muscles of your throat like armour;
and are simply sitting there, with the endurance of a
tired horse after the labour of
singing out to the end all your grief and hunger.
I swear: by the photo, and your delicate pointed
elbows, which are as child-like as the smile of surprise
that death uses to lure children to itself and leaves
as mark upon their faces for evidence.
I swear: by the painful burden of remembering
how I gulped your airless grief from the
breathless rush of your lines, and had to
keep clearing my throat until it bled.
Yes, by your own presence, which I have stolen,
burgled, taken for myself, as if forgetting that
you belong to God, who cannot get enough of you;
and by that starved emaciation which
killed you at the end with its rat tooth.
I swear: by the blessed Motherland herself, even if
she grossly abandoned you like an orphan;
and your beloved African, that great genius of
kindness, whose own end was unkind, now
as a statue watching over small children.
By those children! And the Tversky Boulevard!
And your own sad rest in Paradise, where
there is neither trade nor torment for you!
I swear: to kill that Yelabuga, your
Yelabuga, so that our grandchildren
can sleep soundly. Old women may still frighten
them at nights, not knowing the power of her
'Sleep little child, quietly, quietly, for
blind Yelabuga is coming to catch you.'

And with all her tangle of legs truly she will
hasten towards me crawling with horrible speed.
But I shall bring my boot down on her
tentacles without saying any more, and
put my weight on my heel, and my toe-cap into
the back of her neck, and keep it there.
Then the green juice of her young will burn
the soles of my feet with their poison, but I'll
hurl the egg that ripens in her tail
into the earth, that bottomless earth!
And not say a word of the porch in the photograph.
I will not speak of Marina's homeless death.
I swear it. Even while in
the dark, and in the stench of silt,
with the toads in the well about her, she
has one yellow eye fixed in my direction:
The Yelabuga
swears her own oath—to kill me!

NIGHT

Now on three sides the darkness grows deeper
    with the coming of the dawn, and still my
hand has no courage to reach through the solid
    air to the white paper on the table.

For reason cannot honestly resist my
    sense of limitation! Now I cannot
let my hand write any of those careless
    phrases that once gave me joy.

In darkness there are always many meanings;
    it is easy to mistake the euphoria of
midnight, and a burning head that comes from
    slackness and caffeine—for sharp intelligence.

But evidently I have not damaged my
    brain altogether with my insane vigils.
I understand excitement is no merit,
    however hot; I do not think it talent.

It would be sinful to ignore that misery! Yet
    the temptation is sweet. How small and innocent
a gesture: to destroy the anonymity of night, and
    call all things within it by their right names.

Even as I try to keep my hand still
    each object flirts with me, and shows its
own beauty, I am invited with
    every movement now to render homage

to each thing, convinced of my love,
    whose small voice growls and begs
to have its soul celebrated in song—
    for which it needs my voice.

And I want to thank the candle, and to have
   its lovely light known everywhere, I would
offer tireless epithets as
   caresses. And yet I fall silent.

Under this torture of numbness, what pain—
   not to confess even with one word
the splendour of everything my love looks
   upon from darkness with stern eyes.

Why should I be ashamed? Aren't I free in
   an empty house, in a flood of snow, to
write, however poorly? at least to name
   the house, the snow, and the blue window?

A sheet of paper is defenceless: I pray
   God to keep me modest. Here I sit
before a clear and most ingenuous candle that
   lights my face now floating into sleep.

'For how many years'

For how many years along this street of mine have I
   overheard those footsteps—of my friends leaving.
And the darkness outside my window draws pleasure
   in witnessing every sluggish departure.

That is your stern character, Solitude, as
   you flash an iron compass; how coldly
now do you close your circle round me
   without attending to my useless protest.

Summon me, then, with some reward, since I
   have become your creature, and console myself
with your favours; let me rest against you
   and wash myself in the pale blue of your frost.

In your forest, on my toes, allow me to
   reach the slow peak of one strained gesture in
your foliage, and raise the leaves to my face
   so I may feel—to be desolate is a blessing.

Give me the quiet of your libraries,
   severe melodies in concert halls;
wise power—that is the way we forget
   those who are dead and those not yet alive.

So I shall learn wisdom and sadness together,
   and things will yield their hidden meanings up;
even Nature leaning on my shoulder
   may reveal her childish secrets to me.

But out of all the darkness, tears, and the
   forgetting of what is lost for ever,
the fine features of my friends will
   appear briefly to me, before dissolving.

Twelve lyrics from
RAIN

   I.

All morning I've had this Rain around me.
   Rudely, I kept on saying: Leave me alone!
So it drew back, but soon there it was again
   as sad and loving as a little daughter.

Rain. On my back. Stuck there like a wing.
   I reproached it: Here, you
   shameless, useless thing!
Think of the tears of some market gardener
   and water the flowers.
What do you find in me?

Meanwhile a heatwave was burning everywhere
   which the Rain ignored. And kept on until
there were children whirling all around me
   as if I were some kind of water-sprinkler.

Then I became crafty. Went in a café.
   Sat myself down at a quiet corner table.
But there was the Rain again. Through the glass.
   Motioning towards me, like a beggar.

So I went outside. And at once my face
   felt a wet slap. Immediately
(sorry and bold together) the Rain licked
   my lips, smelling warm as a wet puppy.

I must have looked stupid. As I
   tied a damp headscarf round my neck.
The Rain sat splayed on my shoulders like
   a monkey.
And the town was embarrassed by the whole thing.

While the Rain was delighted to find me helpless.
    It tickled my ear gently with a child's finger. And
all the while everywhere else dried out.
    Except me. I was soaked to the skin.

II.

But I had an invitation to a house, where
    decorous people would be waiting for me,
a house with floors of amber water and
    a candelabra like a moon above them.

And I wondered: What shall I do with this Rain?
    It doesn't seem to intend to go away.
It will make a mess on the floor. And ruin the carpets.
    They won't even let me in if I bring it with me.

So I spoke to it firmly: Look, as you imagine
    I'm kind, but everything has a limit.
Absolutely: You can't come any further.
    At this the Rain looked up at me like an orphan.

—Damn you then. Come! I said:
    Though I don't understand what love holds us together.
A curse on this most peculiar weather!
    Forgiven, the Rain went skipping on ahead.

III.

My host's invitation was something of
    an undeserved honour. However, I
appeared, dripping water like a beaver,
    and rung his bell at six o'clock precisely.

The Rain was hiding somewhere at my back.
Tickling as it sadly breathed down my neck.

Steps. Peephole. Pause. A lock turns.
I began to apologize: I've brought this Rain.

Do you think perhaps it could wait outside in the porch?
since it's much too wet, and too long anyway
to get into a room?
—What? said my astonished
host, and went white in the face.

IV.

And I had loved that house, always, for
   the dance of lightness that was everywhere
and because elbows caught on no sharp corners
   there, and no knives slashed at people's fingers.

I loved it all. The slow rustle of
   the hostess' silk, and the scarf over her face,
And best of all, I loved that sleeping beauty
   captive in the sideboard: crystal glass,

there, with the seven colours of the spectrum; it was
   lifeless and lovely in its transparent coffin.
But I could not dream of it . . . The ritual of
   greetings, began, formal as any opera.

V.

To put it mildly, the mistress of that house would
   never have bothered to hide her dislike of me,
except for the fear of being thought old-fashioned.
   that restrained her, which was perhaps a pity.

—How *are* you? (And how could
   so haughty a slender throat hold back the thunder?)
—Thank you, I answered hastily: I feel
   like a sow that's been wallowing in the mud.

(I don't know what came over me. I meant
to say with some polite
gesture: I'm fine.
And much better for seeing you again.)

But she began to speak at once:
You know, it's a disgrace, for someone like you, with so
                              much talent
to walk so far. In all this rain!
Then everyone started to shout together.
—Bring her up to the fire! To the fire with her!

And once upon a time in another age
it could have happened to a beating drum
in the market place, with music perhaps and jeers
you would have cried:
To the fire, with her, to the fire!

—Hello then, and leap up at me, Fire!
    Brother, dog of many tongues, now lick
my hands in your great tenderness.
    For you are the Rain also. Your burn is wet!

—Your monologue is rather peculiar,
    my host said tartly.
—But never mind, blessings on green sheets!
    There's always charm in a new generation.

—Don't listen to me, I'm delirious, I said.
    It's all the fault of the Rain. All day it's
been pursuing me everywhere, like a devil.
    It's only the Rain that's getting me into trouble.

Then, suddenly, through the window I saw
    my faithful Rain, sitting alone and crying.
And two tears swam into my eyes, and they
    were the last traces of water left in me.

VI.

Now, glass in hand, another woman guest, who
 looked as vague as a pigeon on a cornice,
asked me in a voice refined and waspish
 —Tell me, is it true your husband's rich?

—Is he? I don't know. Not specially.
 Yes, I suppose, work comes so easily
to him. But may I tell you a secret?
 There's something incurably poor in me.

And then my tongue ran away with me,
 —Did you know? I've taught him to cast
spells, on anything of value, so it turns
 into a circle of water, a weasel   or grass.

I'll show you how it's done. Give me your ring.
 We'll soon take that star out of its setting.
(But of course, she wouldn't let me have it
 and turned away from me like a stunned thing.)

—And I want you to know something else,
 I yelled after her, my tongue on fire.
(as though the rain still had control of me)
—My deepest urge is to fall dead in the gutter.

VIII.

Meanwhile to amuse the guests, some
 new family show was about to begin;
they were letting into the sitting room
a lace-clad silver cloud of children.

Hostess, please forgive me! I am evil.
 I've lied and behaved badly. Now I see
from your lips, like those of a glass blower
 a bottle of the purest glass appear,

a wholly-filled vessel of your spirit:
    your child, who is most delicately cast,
the outline of his body firm and even.
    I knew nothing, do not judge me harshly.

Your savage genius must be falling, hostess,
    into despair, day and night to be
forced to lower that monstrous head of his
    over this child, over this son of yours.

The Rain summoned my lips down to her hand
and I wept:
—Forgive me, please forgive,
your eyes are pure, and you must understand.

IX.

Meanwhile the children struck up in chorus nearby

In times like these we have
    to have some kind of laugh.
Ha. Ha. There was a certain Jew
    and this Jew had a wife.

His wife would puff and blow
    and laboured hard and long
to make a little penny grow
    the size of a great house.

New little metal piece
    you ripen like a fruit
and rise up as the sun must rise
    to decorate the sky.

All this is just in play
    our turn and party trick.
What fun! And yet how grim to be
    brought up in this century.

We're only children now
    but grow up in our sleep
as little copper coins grow
    inside the treasury.

All our parental sins
    we have redeemed: Hurrah!
Vulgarity is not a sin,
It gives a cosy mind.

From anger and from pain
    it proves our saviour:
and so we bend to kiss your
    velvet hem, great Queen.

X.

Then laziness like an illness unfolded me
    and my arms moved strangely from my shoulders,
as I kept my glass warm in my hand like a bird
    and its open beak went: peep-peep. Straight at her.

Hostess, have you ever felt remorse
    bending over your son, asleep in the morning
as you fed the milk of your poisoned breast
    into his greedy mouth   that open wound?

Suppose that in him, as in an egg of pearl,
    slept a coiled spring of music?
hidden like a rainbow in a white bud?
    Or like the muscle of beauty in a face?

As in Sashenko, slept unawakened Blok?
    You she-bear, to give yourself what pleasure
did you go hunting with your hungry teeth
    into your cub's fur to crack God like a flea?

XI.

The hostess poured me out another cognac.
  —You're feverish. Warm yourself at the fire.
Farewell, my Rain!
It is so sweet and so full of pleasure,
to feel the tip of my tongue in this cold tingle.

How strangely this wine smells of roses.
Wine—I think only you are blameless.
The atom of the grape is split in me
and so begins the war of the two roses.

Spirit of wine, I am your delinquent
prince, tied between two bent trees.
Tear me apart! Without fear! One crack
and death will separate me from myself.

And now I am bigger and more tender.
Look—I am as kindly as a clown.
I am cast at your feet and bowing down
and already your doors and windows feel like cages.

Lord, what strange goodness, I feel now.
Hurry! While I weep here. On my knees.
I love you. Only a cripple's shyness
whitens my cheeks, and gives my lips their twist.

How can I serve you by one action?
Please hurt me, at least spare me no pain.
Here is my skin, stretched out with space for wounds, and
waiting as a canvas for paint.

I love you without measure, without shame.
And my embrace is round, as the sky itself.
We all share the same source. We are brothers.

Rain, my child. Come here, straightaway!

XII.

Then a shiver ran down every spine
  and in quiet darkness the hostess screamed
as orange marks like rust suddenly
  appeared in streaks upon the white ceiling.

And down poured the Rain. They caught at it
  with tins, pushed it with brooms and brushes.
It escaped. And flew up in their cheeks
  or formed like liquid cataracts in their eyes.

It danced a strange and surprising can-can,
  and rang playfully on the restored crystal.
Then the house snapped its vicious jaws
  over it. Like a man-trap, tearing muscle.

The rain with a look of love and longing even as it
  soiled the floor, crawled to me on its belly;
even while men, lifting their trouser legs,
  kicked at it, or jabbed it with their heels.

They captured it with a floor-cloth and then
squeamishly wrung it out in the lavatory.
Until in a voice made suddenly hoarse and wretched
I shouted out:
—Don't touch. It belongs to me.

It was alive, like a child or an animal.
Now may your children live in torment and misery.
Blind people, whose hands know nothing of mystery
  why have you chosen to stain the Rain in blood?

The lady of the house whispered to me:
—Remember,
you will have to answer for all this.
I burst out laughing:
I know what I shall answer!
You are disgusting. Now please let me pass.

I looked so wretched — passers by were alarmed.
So I kept on saying
—Never mind. Forget it.
Even this episode will soon pass.
And on the parched asphalt
kissed the last drop of water.

For now the bare earth had become white hot,
and the sky-line around the city was pink.
The panic-stricken bureau of weather forecasts
made no promise of any other downpour.

CHAPTERS FROM A POEM

I'll start far away: from there, not here;
from that end which is also a beginning.
From an ordinary world, which means a world
where you find whatever you're expecting.
> There was a wood, like a kitchen garden,
> as small as one, though holding far more. It
> was a place of childish whims, where
> everything existed with its opposite.

In a small clearing, of total silence,
stood a house: an ordinary house. This meant
a woman shook her head over it, and
saw the lamps were lit in the early evening.
> Work was no harder there than a writing lesson
> and someone—we didn't know who—was
> praying alone under the heavens for
> the forgiveness of our imperfect thoughts.

And because in the balance between good and
evil, he took on guilt himself, the earth flew
carelessly as it wished, just as long as
the candle burned over that table;
> there could be forgiveness of ignorant people
> and liars—no difference between them—he atoned
> for all of us in front of that white light:
> so we were able to forget about it.

But when the blank he left rose over
the world, about sunrise, Nature
felt the shock—and with a jerk
had to shift the weight of all our bodies.
> Infinity observed us, with surprise,
> gathered as we were in our poor crowd:
> knowing there was no one any longer
> to make up for the ugliness of our lives.

To that house many people went. And
two boys, in striped shirts, entered
that front garden where raspberries were
darkening in the dark—without fear.

> I was once nearby, but I'm
> a stranger to the modern habit of
> easy contact, the familiar way
> of using people's first names.
> So in the evening, I was proud enough to
> look at the house, and pray towards
> the building and the garden and the car.
> I did not even say his name aloud.
> > It was autumn: and there was to be
> > no summer to come, but at that
> > time we did not yet know the
> > circle of the year would not be round.
> Sternly I avoided meeting him, walked off
> into the trees. And inevitably
> found myself looking into his
> spacious face and hearing his drawled speech.
> > But do I dare rhyme with your name before me?
> > No.

He came out suddenly from a wretched thicket of Peredelkino's trees, late one evening, in October. It was more than two years ago. He was dressed in the coarse but tidy outfit of a hunter: blue raincoat, boots, and white knitted mittens. Something between tenderness for him and my own pride kept me from looking into his face. I saw only the bright white flashes of his hands, at the corners of my eyes; and that blinded me.

He said, 'Oh, hello. I've been told about you, and I recognized you at once.' And then, suddenly, with unexpected intensity he implored me, 'Please forgive me! I have to telephone this very moment.'

He was just about to enter a small building of some kind, but he turned sharply, and out of the pitch dark I was suddenly struck, or rather *splashed*, by the brilliant whiteness of his face: his forehead and cheekbones seemed luminescent in the weak moonlight. I was seized by an icy-sweet, Shakespearian chill, seeing him. He asked, 'Aren't you cold? It's nearly November!' And then seeming embarrassed, he backed away clumsily through the door.

Leaning against the wall, I heard him speaking, as if with my body, as though suddenly deaf. He was speaking to someone with great love in his voice, as if he were making excuses for himself. With my back and my hands, I absorbed the strange tones: the singing of the phrases, the kindly eastern mumble that turned into an indistinct trembling and rumbling through the board partition. I, and the house, and the surrounding bushes all fell inadvertently into the love his rounded and delicate voice generated.

Then he came out, and walked a little way with me over ground that was overgrown with stumps of trees and branches, crossed with hedges, and altogether extremely difficult to walk on. But he managed to walk over the uneven ground easily; at home, although an abyss had closed over us, with stars cheaply sparkling above, and a cavity where the moon should have been. We walked together through the crudely placed, comfortless trees.

He said, 'Why don't you ever come round? Sometimes interesting people visit me—you won't be lonely. Come. Tomorrow.'

But because I was feeling faintly giddy I answered almost rudely: 'Thank you. I'll drop in some time, without fail.'

Out of the forest, as from the wings
of a theatre, he became grandiloquent
with no intention of overwhelming
anyone: he threw out his arms!
    Then he was both actor and himself,
    part of the ancient stage of lovely speaking.
    As a play begins! And the lights go out! Blue
    phosphorus glimmers through the words.
—Hello, it's nearly November, aren't you
cold? That is all he said.
As if he was playing the part of
universal love to people and animals.
    And that is how to play. With joy yet
    seriously. To the point of tears. For ever.

>   Without cunning. He played like animals
>   or children play with the world as they lap milk.
> —Farewell. Singing like this is not common
> unless in front of footlights, there
> they use song to end their monologue of
> a drama whose issue is death or love.
>> The curtain is down already! The darkness lit!
>> But everything is not over: Drop in tomorrow.
>> How hospitable is that tone of
>> excitement, it belongs only to Georgians.
> Can there be another such house
> on earth—I don't know! But it seems
> impossible to enter. Always carelessly, I
> did not call, that day or any after.
>> I wept among the stars, the trees
>> and country cottages, After the show, in
>> the darkening stalls, as children cry
>> much, at their first taste of loss.

He used to maintain: among the
greenhouses and icebergs, just
south of Paradise, (to the
noise of a child's whistle)
a second universe rises called Tblisi.

My eyes burn, my hands are cold.
My love, I am weeping for Tblisi.
For that miraculous concave cornice
God holds up by caprice
above this earth.

Mist hurts my eyes, for all
my errors began there,
in that half-circular town which is
like an unsteady smile on the blessed mouth of Tamar.

I do not know for what pleasure
it closed its oval over me,
kissed and bewitched me completely,
and for life and death made me,
the eternal prisoner of Metekha.

Oh, if I had not drunk of
the waters of Kura!
Not drunk the waters of
Aragva!
And not known the sweetness
of their poison!
Not fallen face down on
those grasses!

If I could still return
your gifts, generous Georgian!
But it is too late. The drink has
been sipped, and the intoxication
is eternal. God sees my
dream of you is deep as the
valley of the Alazan river.

'You were sleeping'

You were sleeping, today, while I was looking about us
into the shadows, a horseman on patrol.
It was then I understood exactly how late it was:
how death is waiting on stage, and how everything passes,
and though it looks innocent to scribble these lines
poetry is no longer private as prayer.
This generation demands performance. The guilt of that
I take on without the gift or desire for it.
For your sake I take on the shame of pretence
so that in me may be seen some hint of the past,
of how it might be with Marina and Anna alive
when poetry and conscience could live together.
So now in my throat, which is clean and clumsy,
an echo sounds of the ancient Russian word.
I have become an ambiguous, homely ghost
of two poets whose lives can never return.
I have inherited the tenderness that is theirs,
as much as I can bear, for more would murder me.
I understand how little I'm worth myself.
Yet, God knows, something links me to my listeners.
Perhaps the most virtuous thing would be silence itself,
which is the only certain way to keep lips from lying.
If that's impossible, then take away my voice
my last voice, and allow me to live honourably
until I leave everyone   whenever that may be!
At least my spirit is without cunning,
remains vigilant, and does not choose
the favours of this world, without fear of the next.
So I burn to speak truth, and I serve deceit
and must while I have life and energy.